Journey Of Miracles

PATTI SPENCER

ISBN:0692212965
ISBN-13: - 978-0692212967

DEDICATION

To all my friends that have encouraged me to write my story and have prayed for me in times of need, to Minister Donn that has insisted I write it and to my children that had part in my journey of miracles, this book is dedicated.

CONTENTS

ACKNOWLEDGMENTS

Our appreciation to Diana Barkley for her cover design.

CHAPTER 1

THE FIRST MIRACLE

Some people don't believe in miracles. The word "miracle" has been changed from the meaning given in Acts of the Apostles to mean demonstrations of the mind scientists and occultists of today. What we called miracles in the 50's were the same kind you read about in the book of Acts. A few very popular evangelists through the years have remained known, such as Amy McPherson that built Angelus Temple, Kathryn Kuhlman and others. But the many thousands that saw great miracles take place in their lives have died and left no stories behind them.

The greatest of the miracles and healings of those days were not as rare as believed. My story is not exceptional but is only one of the thousands that could have been told of ministers that traveled the countryside leaving in their wake healings and miracles that are not known today.

My very first miracle happened when I about five years old. My great grandfather was alive when I was little and some of my fondest memories are when he'd rock me in his rocking chair and sing gospel songs with some of the gospel singers on the radio. He would read out of his worn bible, stories of angels and stories of miracles that Jesus and his disciples had.

Granddaddy was the son of what one might call today a Billy Graham of 1800's. As a simple circuit riding preacher man, he was attributed with over 5000 converts but he only baptized about three thousand of them as he told the rest they were not ready, to go back and pray some more!

One of the funniest stories Granddaddy told me about him, that I wanted him to tell me again and again, was about the Methodist preacher. He went into a town to have a brush arbor meeting and there was already a Methodist church there. The Methodist preacher came out to the meeting place and told him that there was already a church there and they did not need the devil coming in trying start another one.

At that, my great-great grandfather got down on his knees and started praying. The Methodist asked him what he was praying about. He got up, told him that he always prayed the prayer of repentance before he sinned, to make sure God would hear him and forgive him. Then he gave the Methodist a good left to the jaw and sent him tumbling down the hill, picked up his Bible and went into the crowd and started to preach.

There's a few chapters in some books in the Southern Baptist central library about him, and in one book it tells that on his death bed he said he had missed his calling. He should have evangelized instead of just being a circuit pastor and building churches. Today we would call that an Apostle of Jesus Christ.

One of the books with some chapters about him is called, "Pioneer Tennessee Baptist Preachers" and there is another but I do not know the name of it at this time. I do have a copy of the chapter from one of them that tells the various churches he established in Tennessee, North Carolina and Virginia areas. He was a licensed minister with what was then called "The Christian Union" and the Southern Baptist churches took in his churches under their denomination later when they were established.

One of those churches was called, "Fire Baptized Liberty Baptist" in Lebanon, Virginia which he pastored thirteen years. With three other Baptist

Ministers he went into Sodom, Tennessee and preached revival where no other preachers had been allowed to come. He was powerful to defend the Baptist cause in debates with other denominational ministers whenever he had a chance.

I was not an ordinary child. I had been very ill since birth. My mother had died when I was three days old with Toxemia poisoning and that could have had something to do with it. Since I was so little I do not know what all was wrong with me by medical name but I was not allowed to run and play with other children. The doctor had told my grandmother that I might drop over dead if I became over-exhausted. I had to take several doses of the most terrible tasting medicines they ever invented and could eat only a very few well prepared foods. We would call them baby foods today.

My grandmother took me often to the Medical Arts Hospital in Dallas, Texas for tests. I remember going through the revolving doors kicking and screaming and going through some very painful and horrifying to a little child tests ever so often. Then Grandmother would sit in the doctor's office with me and place several bottles of medicine on his desk and he would write new prescriptions. I thought he must have found new medicines that tasted worse and wanted me to have them!

One of the happy times of my life was on Sundays when Granddaddy would take me to the old First Baptist Church downtown which was then just an old wooden building with a balcony and the family often talked about his plumbing the building when it was new and he didn't ask for a dime payment not even for the plumbing. He had the first Plumbing shop in the little Texas town where I was born. Grandaddy loved the Lord and he loved the church. He was one of the Elders as I understood it and in those days they even said "Amen" at times out loud.

I would go to Sunday school and I enjoying getting to be with other children and then we would go up the stairs to the balcony where Granddaddy liked to sit for the regular church service. One morning they had a visiting preacher and he was preaching a revival. I believe his name was Rev Pruitt from the First church in Dallas. I've heard he was the one that took Billy Graham's confession of faith. It was the first time I understand an altar call and I got away from Granddaddy and ran to the altar. He was yelling for someone to stop that little girl as the Baptists do not believe a child of that age is old enough to know what they are doing.

The evangelist stepped down from the podium and said,

"Let that little girl through to Jesus she knows what she is doing and so does Jesus!"

I will never forget those words or what happened next. He did something Baptist preachers do not ordinarily do, he placed his hand on my head and I felt a fire come down through my body that I know today to be the Holy Spirit the disciples received on the day of Pentecost. That's one way it's felt but not always. Nor does one always have to speak in tongues as some denominations insist. The Bible does not specifically say that it is necessary. It simply states it happened to the disciples but did not specifically say to one hundred percent of them. Some people are more demonstrative than others. The problem with denominations is that they read they own interpretations into the scriptures instead of just reading the literal Word of God and accepting it as it is.

I go back to that day in memory as the day I met Jesus Christ in person and was "born again" according to his word. It was not long afterward we made another trip to Dallas for the tests and the new nasty medicines! Another day I shall never forget.

I watched the doctor as my Grandmother placed all the bottles on his desk for him to look at and he picked up his trash basket, swept them all off into it and told my Grandmother I needed no more medicine, I was well and could now run and play with all the other children and could eat anything I wanted to eat.

He also said I could now go to school as they did not think I would die before I finished. As of today, I'm eighty-three and still going strong as the energizer battery! And I give no credit to the medical profession but to Jesus Christ and that Baptist preacher that went against his church rules and took a little five year old girl's confession of faith in Jesus Christ seriously, may he rest in peace in the Kingdom of Heaven. God bless you, Brother Pruitt!

CHAPTER 2

MY MAMA SUTTIE

This story cannot be told without telling about Mama Suttie. She was the only Mama I ever had. My mother died three days after I was born and I didn't have a father that I know. It was claimed my mother ran off and married a coal miner from West Virginia but he gave me to my grandmother to raise and later when I was a teen ager and ran off to go see him I was told he was not my real father but only married my mother to give me a name.

I never knew who my father was but Grandmother worked out and lived with her father and mother who were still alive and they hired Mama Suttie to watch after me and do some of the housework. My great grandmother did her own cooking. Sometimes Mama Suttie would wear her long white missionary dress and I'd get hold of the hem and follow her around singing and speaking in tongues just like she did.

I don't know if I really had the Holy Ghost back then or I was just imitating her. But I remember Granddaddy used to tell me to stop talking in that Dutch like Mama Suttie as he couldn't understand either of us and God couldn't either!

I know today that God does understand and gave us the prayer language in tongues so the devil could not know what our Spirit was praying to God. That's one reason we have the baptism of the Holy Spirit today so we can have a prayer language that only God can understand. Though the carnal mind does not understand and medical field cannot understand unless they are born again and filled with the Holy Spirit themselves.

Mama Suttie used to take me to her house when she had prayer meetings and I remember them making a circle around me, laying hands on my head and calling the name of Jesus. This could have been where my healing came from, as it was a miracle healing whoever prayed the prayer for it.

Several years ago I was told by one of the mothers of the Church of God in Christ when I told this story about Mama Suttie at a District meeting, that the Church here in my town where I was raised was started through those very prayer meetings at my Mama Suttie's house. I do not doubt that's where I first received the baptism of the Holy Ghost.

I always remembered my Mama Suttee but she left me sometime before my healing, and she never knew about it. They moved up about thirty miles away from us and it was in late 60's, when my fourth child was born, I was staying here with my Grandmother, in the same house where I was born, when I came out of the hospital.

My baby was very ill but the doctor did not even share with me how ill because she had contacted a disease that no infant that young had lived. I had nurses' training and he felt I was capable of caring for her and told me what to do and let me take her home. He said to make sure she stayed at constant temperature as at that age to contact a cold could mean pneumonia and she could die. He was preparing me for the worst.

I had been up with her night and day and I fell asleep and one our Texas Northers came up in the night and I woke up and it was cold and was having trouble breathing. She was very pale and just gasping for breath and I heard some talking in the kitchen, it was early morning, just after daylight and I went in to get Grandmother and there was this old black lady in a long white dress sitting there. Grandmother said,

"I bet you don't know who this is!" And I answered,

"Yes, I do, it's my Mama Suttie!"

I grabbed her and hugged her as she got up to hug me and I asked her if she prayed for people I wanted her to come pray for my baby I knew she was going to die."

And she did, and she had me touch her and she held my hand and lifted her other one to heaven and started speaking in her Holy Ghost tongue. The power came through her like an electric shock and went into my baby and you could see the fever leave through her head, the color came back to her and she started breathing normal and fell asleep.

There's more to the story. And I have to add a bit of preaching here. I do not believe in the prosperity ministry as they preach it today. I do think a man/woman can tell you God is going to do something for you if you give them money for their ministry. I do believe we cannot out give God and if God tells us to give we better do it. God told me to give her my last five dollars.

She told me it was her bus fare back home as she said Jesus told her three times to come to little Patsy as she needed her. She argued with him and said that I would be married and living somewhere far off and would not be at the old house. He told her I was there and I needed her. God can talk to us if we listen. He doesn't talk in some booming outward voice but he could. But most of the time he speaks in the still small voice within.

I have heard the audible voice of God. When I dedicated my life to Jesus Christ at church camp when I was fourteen years old, I heard an audible voice say, "Preach MY Gospel" and I knew it was my Jesus. Though I never heard of a woman preacher at that time there were some and it was few years later I heard of the first one and then I knew it was true, I was truly called to the ministry of preaching.

I've been made fun of because I was a woman but women have the same callings as men as the Bible says, "there is neither man nor woman in the Lord" and Paul said it himself. And I have a message on some of the few other scriptures that men have gone to seed on to keep women quiet in the church and I'd love to preach it anywhere. I may put it on a video later.

So finally Mama Suttie told Jesus alright she would come but she didn't have money for a round trip ticket and he'd have to get her back home and she knew if it was truly God sent her he would get her back home, and he did, with my last five dollars and some of it was for the baby's milk.

So Mama prayed and she prophesied that God would provide the milk for the baby and she would never be without milk, and she was not. Later, my husband and I went to Italy on assignment, he was Air Force, and where we lived the milk truck that came down from another place often broke down and our commissary was out of milk. But my baby never was without milk as someone would just come over, knock on the door, tell us they knew we had a little baby and they had extra milk and wanted us to have it! That's just like Jesus! You cannot out give God.

CHAPTER 3

LITTLE ELIJAH

I have considered telling this story, as it's rather funny. I get a good laugh out of telling it and my Grandmother used to tell it to people and thought was so cute. I've heard her tell it a million times. So I will have to add it to my book.

Mama Suttie's husband got a job in another town and they moved away. I was just heart broken as I loved my Mama Suttie and she loved me and I knew it. So Grandmother had to hire someone else to watch after me and do some of the housework so the only one she could find was a younger black girl. This girl was not at all patient with me nor my Granddaddy and Granddaddy didn't like her either. She would get a switch after me and scare me with it and they told her I was not supposed to be upset as I could die and she didn't seem to care if I died or not.

My Grandmother's brother lived with us and worked. He was stone death and could not hear it thunder. We all had to yell when we talked. He wanted his white shirts washed and starched just right. This new girl had washed outside, in a big black pot with a fire under it. She had a line full of white, starched shirts. Back in the early 30's there was no such thing as a clothes dryer and we hung clothes to dry out on a line, stretched from a pole to a pole.

This girl got after me with a switch for some reason and I told her she better not do that and she said she was anyway, she didn't care if I dropped dead or not! So I told her if she switched me again I was going to pray like

Elijah and have it rain on her white shirts and blow them all down in the dirt! Now I knew about Elijah as Granddaddy had told me the story of Elijah and how he prayed and it rained. So I took a stick and I twirled around a few times, pointed my stick to the sky and said,

"Rain, rain, rain come and blow those white shirts all down in the dirt!"

Then I ran and hid from her. It was not too long until the sky began to get black and the worst storm I ever saw came up. The winds blew, the clothesline broke and all those white shirts went down in the dirt!

The way Grandmother told it, she was coming home from work in town, the rain had stopped and this girl was coming down the road fast as she could walk. Grandmother asked her why she was leaving early, where was little Patsy, as that's what they called me when I was little.

The girl told her she was not keeping that little witch another minute, she was afraid of me. She said I prayed, a storm came up and blew all the white shirts in the mud so she just left them there and was going home and not coming back! She never did and my next Nanny didn't threaten me with a switch either! I think word got around that I was a little witch!

That's the story of little Elijah and the white shirts.

CHAPTER 4

MY MISSIONARY CALLING

My family, other than my great grandfather, were not what one would call Christian, though they claimed to be. They were mad at the Baptist church over some things and they did not go to church. So when Granddaddy passed away I didn't get to go anymore. They never gave God any credit for my healing though they knew Mama Suttie would take me to her prayer meetings to be prayed for. Back in those days, the Baptists did not believe in healing as the Pentecostals do and I do not suppose they do today. But it was very obvious my healing was not through the medical profession.

My neighbors would take me to Sunday school when my Grandmother would let me go with them. They went to the First Christian so that's where I went. Soon as I was big enough to walk on my own I went to Church every Sunday. Back in the 1930's it was safe to walk on the street when you were little. The church was just a few blocks away so I got to go when I was big enough to go by myself.

I went to church camp as a teen ager and I dedicated my life to the Lord when I was fourteen years old at Denison Dam, at the Baptist camp. I was kneeling by the lake as they towed a burning cross across the water and we sang "Follow, I Will Follow Thee O Lord". Several of us dedicated our lives at the time to full time Christian work. I heard a voice call me to the ministry. If you had been kneeling beside me you probably would not have heard it but it was so clear to me it was like an audible voice and he said,

'Preach MY Gospel."

And the "MY" was very accented. I had read the Bible since I had learned to sound out letters before I started to school and the first book I started to read was the Holy Bible. I got as far as Genesis chapter two before I gave up but I started reading it again as soon as I learned more about reading. It's been my favorite book ever since and each time I read it through I see more than I saw before and different things are revealed.

The Bible is not a book like a history book or a chemistry textbook. It is a layered book and each scripture has more than one interpretation. The problem is that people see one thing and they do not see the depth of the scripture. They start doctrines and churches based on how they see the scriptures.

The scriptures really cannot be understood with the carnal mind as Paul tells us that "The carnal mind is enmity with God and cannot please God". We have to have the Holy Spirit of Truth to lead us into all truth.

When we got back home the young people were given the service on Sunday night. I was asked to speak on the dedication service. When it was over a dear sister came up to me and said,

"If our church believed in women ministers you would make a good one as the speech you gave brought tears to many eyes."

That was a sign to me that the words had come directly from the Lord. I had never heard of a woman minister so I did not tell anyone I heard that call to preach. I simply said I dedicated my life to service of Christ and wanted to be a missionary.

My Grandmother was very opposed to this. In fact, when I wanted to be baptized she did not want me to go and made an excuse she could not go with me as she was having her teeth pulled. She did not have to go with me but she did not let me go that night. The Pastor got mad at me because he had prepared for the baptism service and I did not show up to be baptized.

The church would have helped me go to the university but my grandmother was so opposed to it I finally gave up. The reason I did not go on to be in full time Christian service is another reason. I am not telling this on anyone that is alive as this man was much older than I and I'm sure he is gone now to be with the Lord. He was a Sunday school teacher of the Men's Sunday school and always said the prayer to open the Sunday morning service. I just did not feel he was sincere.

Once a year they would come to the High School and put on what was called a "Minstrel Show". This was where they painted their faces black with soot and made fun of black people. Now I loved my Mama Suttie like my own mother and I did not appreciate them doing this. I did not believe his prayers reached the ceiling.

I know that's no excuse but the persecution from my own family and my music teachers was a lot for a young girl with no one to support my belief. My grandmother had my music teacher talk to me of the horrors of missionary work and all that could happen and what I would have to do but the actual turning point was the minstrel show. I surely hope they don't have those kind of things anymore.

Parents, do not stop your children when they have a call of God! You do not know what might happen to them out in life. I had no one to give me any support and backing so I just faded out of the picture. All I did was read the Bible and I did not run around like other girls at that time.

I asked my Pastor one time why it was we do not pray for the sick and believe in healings and miracles as Bible says the early church did. He told me when I went to college and studied Bible they would explain to me that the day of miracles was over. I knew that I had been healed by God as a child even if no one told me I knew that. And so I did not believe the day of miracles was over.

Later when I had received the Holy Ghost and moved back to my hometown I went to a church that was Full Gospel and met an old school mate of mine. She told me she was in that church when she was young but she never mentioned it to me. She never mentioned it to anyone actually and she should have as I might have gone with her and my life turned out differently. I had not heard of a church that believed in miracles, healing, women preachers nor in the baptism of the Holy Ghost at that time. I would have gone there. We don't know how important our witness is as only God knows the hearts.

I have always regretted not going on to TCU and becoming a missionary but later in life I had the chance to do missionary work in more than one foreign country as an Air Force wife and I'll tell about those times later in my story. I suppose that's why I have so many African friends on Facebook. I always wanted to go to Africa to win Mama Suttie's people to the Lord. Our mentors at an early age make such an impression on our lives. I came from a very dysfunctional household. I have envied people that had a Christian upbringing and I tried to give that to my children and the grandchildren as I could. I know how important it is to have an adult believe in your Christian experience. If I had one message for every parent in America and the world it would be, "Go to church somewhere and take your children. They might go back on God and go out into the world but one day they will return to the faith of their parents and their childhood.

My Mama Suttie and my great grandfather Routh were the ones that made the most impression on my life. I love Gospel music, Granddaddy used to love to listen to gospel and the Grand Ole Opry and the gospel singers that went there. I love Gospel singing today. I post as many as I can on Facebook and other places. Granddaddy would sing me to sleep singing "The Old Rugged Cross" and "Amazing Grace" and these things are etched on a child's memory when everything else is forgotten.

Mama Suttie went around the house, working and singing, with me holding on to her long white missionary dress and singing with her. I wanted to wear one of those long white missionary dresses and I got a chance to later in life. I'll be telling that story and more as I go along. I thank God for the teachings I did receive from Mama Suttie and Granddaddy Routh and the Christ love I felt from them both.

CHAPTER 5

MY NEAR DEATH EXPERIENCE

My second child was born in November 1952, at Florence Nightingale Maternity Center at Baylor, Hospital, Dallas, Texas.

At the time of her birth I had been used in an experiment without my permission, by the doctor who informed me it was being done while it was in process. I was not a charity patient but had insurance through my husband's policy from his work. These experiments are done more often than people realize without their permission and should be outlawed as illegal. This was a very serious mistake and almost cost me my life.

The doctor was a woman that was a retired Colonel. My opinion is she wanted to go somewhere so wanted to rush the delivery. The baby came suddenly, I was not dilated and I heard her say,

"I can't stop the blood, I'm loosing her if anyone knows how to pray now would be a good time."

I have asked for the medical records in the past and was informed I'd have to have an attorney to get them. I would advise anyone to be sure of their doctors and make sure they know you do not want to be used in their experiments.

I began in my mind to say the Lord's Prayer. Before I finished, I found myself out of my body and standing in the room, looking at what was happening. They had pushed the gurney over against the wall and only one nurse stood by me.

As far as the doctor was concerned, I had lost all my blood, my vital signs were gone and I was dead. She was not even trying to work with me at all and only one nurse stood by me. The doctor went outside to my Grandmother, Aunt and husband and asked what they wanted done with the body as she told them I was gone and she could do nothing about it.

Immediately after leaving my body a shaft of very white light came down in the room and a beautiful woman with long black hair in a white robe trimmed in gold came down through the Light. She extended her hands toward me and gave me the choice of either going up in the Light with her or staying on earth in my body. At first, I wanted to go with her in the Light, as the experience was so beautiful and peaceful. I was also totally out of pain as the Light surrounded me.

The next memory I have was standing again outside the light in the delivery room and saying, 'I choose to live', which I presume was a decision to come back on earth for my mission was unfinished. My original choice was to go up in the Light with the beautiful Lady so something evidently changed my mind about it during the four hours I was unconscious. The doctors had then told my family if I ever awakened from the coma I was in that I would be nothing but a vegetable.

I have no memory of what happened nor why I was allowed to come back but I believe it's because God was not finished with me and had yet even begun. I have read that sometimes when something is hidden to our memory it will return in another way, perhaps as a dream experience or other type event or vision.

CHAPTER 6

VOICE OF AN ANGEL

As result of what caused my NDE in 1952, the doctor said that I had to have another operation. That I lived through that was another miracle. I know it was an Angel that saved my life.

After the operation I seemed to be doing fine and they put me in a room right across from the nurses' station and left me alone. I'd had a spinal and I woke up and wanted a drink but could not reach the nurses' call button. I heard what I thought was water dripping and I was very much drugged and was unaware I was slowly bleeding to death.

Soon they came and picked me up and I asked where all the blood came from. Immediately a nurse put a pillow over my face and said it was the one in the bed with me. Of course there was no one but I was too drugged to understand.

Next thing I knew I woke up from another operation and they said the resident doctor had saved my life. In the first operation, which was elective repair work for what happened to me that caused the NDE, the doctor had left a blood vessel unattended and I was slowly bleeding to death. The doctor on but saved my life as well as the nurse that found me.

The next day when I was more awake they brought a red headed nurse in to see me. They said she wanted to meet me as she was the one saved my life. She sat down by me and told me this story.

She was working three flights down and she claimed she heard me say clearly to her,

"I am bleeding to death, I am in room so and so, come quickly!"

She did not wait on the elevator but ran up three flights of stairs to my room and found me covered in blood. That's why they got to me in time and saved my life. She did not understand why the nurses right across the hall from me did not hear me calling.

I told her I did not call her and I did not know what my room number was. She said it was like someone standing right by her and talking to her, three flights down. It had to be an Angel that saved my life.

CHAPTER 7

GOSPEL TENT HEALING

I came into the Pentecostal experience through a healing experience. When I had the operation for repair work the doctor removed some polyps and sent them for a biopsy. He told me they were what he called, first cousin to cancer, and if the symptoms came back I had to have an immediate hysterectomy.

I was renting from an older couple at the time while working, and I told them about it. They asked if I believed God still healed today and I told them, yes, I knew he did as I had been healed as a little girl. They wanted me to go with them that night to a tent meeting where people were being healed so I did.

The tent meeting was Rev A.A. Allen and he called out everyone with cancer to run to the altar as the Spirit was there to heal cancer. The people pushed me out in the aisle and told me to run so I did. I stood in the prayer line and passed under him and he laid his hands on my head in the Name of Jesus and went to the next person. I felt nothing and walked around to my seat.

The next morning all symptoms were gone. I went back to the doctor and he was amazed. He said there was nothing wrong with me!

Then I began to seek the baptism of the Holy Spirit in various churches. The first time I heard of the baptism was when I attended the tent meeting where I was healed. I did not receive the baptism in a church. I received it at home kneeling beside my bed one Sunday morning after church services.

When this experience happened to me I felt pulled back out of my body and I could hear myself speaking softly in an unknown tongue.

That is not simply another language spoken on the planet as most of the churches now teach. I have studied five languages and speaking in any foreign language gives me no more power than speaking my native language, English, nor does it anyone else. That is a lie and trick of the devil he has devised to fool the people into thinking they have received the Holy Spirit baptism as on the day of Pentecost.

The Baptism gives us the same power over all the power of the enemy the Disciples of Christ received on the day of Pentecost. Why they were understood by those standing in the streets was that after the initial receiving of the Holy Spirit they were given the gift of knowledge to enable them to speak in other languages to preach the gospel. That is not the sign of the initial infilling of the Holy Spirit. I know it is taught in many churches now but it was not the way it was taught when the outpouring of the Holy Spirit came in healing wave, I know, I was there. Those that did teach it were considered led of the wrong spirit as the Holy Spirit is a very real power and those of us that have felt it and been used by God in miraculous ways understand. There is no power in speaking another language but it is a gift of the Holy Spirit after one receives the initial baptism.

I was with a group that went down into Mexico to preach the gospel one weekend and we were doing some street preaching. Most of those that gathered round us could not understand English. One of the brothers that was preaching began to speak in Spanish very fluently. And some gave their hearts to Jesus Christ through that message. That is the Spirit gift of knowledge in operation. He already had the Baptism of the Spirit.

I heard a testimony once of a young man that had gone into the Soviet Union on official business and had decided to smuggle some bibles to Christians he knew about that wanted the Bible. This was many years ago when the government would not allow Bibles to come in legally. This young man was with another and they were carrying the bibles to the group that held service in secret. They saw Russian police officers approaching.

One said what will we do now we will surely be caught and thrown in jail and perhaps imprisoned. The other one said all we can do is pray and I'm going to pray in my prayer language. When we receive the baptism God gives us a prayer language. This is again not an earth language but we speak it just as we would speak normally and we use it to pray. Because our spirit is praying and speaking to the Universal Creator for things needed that we may not know about and to control the circumstances in our lives. We also pray in our prayer language because the enemy of our soul cannot understand it, but can understand our language.

In fact, Satan speaks all languages fluently and understands them so what good would it do to speak in a language of earth just because you did not know it? Satan knows it and would understand so God has given us a prayer language not known on this planet when we have the reality of the baptism of the Holy Spirit they had on the day of Pentecost. And it works!

He continued to pray aloud as the Russian authority figure came close and spoke something in Russian to him. He just continued to pray as he did not understand him though the one with him did speak some Russian. He continued not to say anything as his friend continued to pray in his prayer language. The Russian said a few more words, smiled, and walked right on by.

When they were some ways away the young man that knew some Russian told his friend,

"I didn't know you spoke such fluent Russian! Why didn't you tell me and that was such good idea. You are very, very wise. They believed you and didn't try to look into the package."

I don't remember exactly what it was he said he told the Russian, it's been a long time since heard that testimony but whatever it was, it was believed and it was not the young man that did it but the Spirit of the Living God!

CHAPTER 8
MY BAPTISM AND FIRST MESSAGE

The Holy Spirit is a very powerful experience though one may not run and jump over benches, it's a very powerful experience that connects one with the power of the Christ. The reason that was done so much back in the early days of the revival of Spirit is because people did not know they could simply receive the power of God and channel it for healing and deliverance of others. There is nothing wrong with emotion.

We are beings that have been given our emotions and we do not want to be robots nor zombies and emotion is not a bad thing. To worship God in any way is still worship, whether we sit quietly in meditation on the scriptures, as I often do, or sing, clap our hands and praise God for his goodness, it is still acceptable with God. We have a choice it's not that one way is wrong and the other right, some are more demonstrative than others. I've always been the quiet type and when I start shouting you can believe there is something to shout about! And sometimes I do that, too.

When I received the baptism I was not overly emotional but I did know something happened to me. I went next door to tell my baby sitter I had received the baptism as I had gone to church with her a few times. She said at once that I had not received anything as when she received the Holy Spirit she shouted all around the church. I was never a very demonstrative person and rather shy and it was not my way.

I went back home rather sadly and I prayed about it. I also prayed about my calling when I was fourteen. I asked God if the calling was still good and I truly had the Pentecostal blessing on my life then give me a place to preach that very night!

I got ready to go to church and I went to one where I'd never been before. I had prayed to be led and I felt led to go to a small store front church in Baytown, Texas. I had heard there were prophets there and I asked God for a sure word of prophesy about my ministry. I went in and services had already started. An old man was in the pulpit praying. I sat down on the back seat and began to speak quietly in my prayer language. The old man looked directly at me, pointed his finger and said,

"Sister, I see you behind the pulpit. Come and preach for me tonight! You are a God called minister."

I never got to the pulpit. I raised my hands and was speaking in the Holy Ghost tongue and I don't know what happened next. When I came to myself people were lying on the floor everywhere speaking in tongues and some were at the altar crying and praying to God.

I was ministering in the gift of knowledge to a young man bound by nicotine and was telling him to take his cigarettes out of his back pocket and lay them on the altar and God would deliver him and he did. That's how the gift of knowledge works. It is not the same as fortune telling or how psychics claim to know the future. It is never used other than for God's holy work, never should a price tag be put upon any type of prayer or work of the Holy Spirit.

When one speaks under the anointing of the Holy Spirit it is always true. The Holy Ghost makes no mistakes.

After the service a man came over and gave me his card. He told me he was a scout for the full gospel business men of Houston and he invited me to come minister for them at their next meeting. He said they were looking for a sign gift ministry like mine and a woman, also, to sponsor big time. That was my big chance and an open door God opened for me and I did not go through it. The reason I won't try to explain. I just listened to the wrong voice and we can do that. I took a lady home that said she had no way She told me that was not God that used me as if it had been God I would have told everyone they must do as her church doctrine taught I order to be saved. I did not believe it as I've always been a Baptist girl and I knew the Bible. We are not saved by our works but saved by the grace of God. That does not mean we should sin, as Paul said to the Romans in chapter 6,

"God forbid, how shall we that are dead to sin, live any longer."

The scriptures tell us clearly it is not by works of righteousness that we are saved but by His grace. I had preached that it was only because of the blood of Jesus shed on the cross that cause our sins to be put away forever. I have always loved the song that goes like this;

"What can wash away our sins, nothing but the blood of Jesus."

That's an old Baptist song I heard often as a very little girl at church with my granddaddy.

The woman preached to me all the way home and said it was all the work of the devil and not God at the service. Yet people testified to being healed and if the devil heals and God does not, then maybe we are worshipping the wrong God? But the devil does nothing but lie, steal and destroy as Jesus said, "The enemy comes to steal, kill and destroy and is a liar and the father of it"!

But I allowed her to hinder me from going through the door the Holy Spirit opened and the very next woman they sponsored country-wide was Kathryn Kuhlman! If you've never heard of Kathryn, she was considered the world's greatest healer. She was acknowledged as a woman of God by the Pope of the Roman church who stood up when she entered his presence and she did not bow nor kiss his hand.

If you've never seen Kathryn's ministry, and she is gone now to be with the Lord, you should try to watch her on a video. She never prayed for anyone, the Spirit of God just moved through the audience and healed people though some that did not even believe in healing. A doctor that came to scoff and find fault with Kathryn was healed of deafness in an ear that had no ear drum. He found that the ear drum was there, a creative miracle of God, and it happened at Kathryn's meeting. I heard him and other doctors testify and some sent their patients to her meeting, some from Mayo clinic were there one night sitting on her front seat. God is real, God is a God of miracles and those miracles can happen to you!

CHAPTER 9

GOD ALWAYS MAKES A WAY

My first marriage was to a boy that had just come out of the service and was an alcoholic and I did not know it until too late. He would get drunk and come home hurt me and the children and I put up with it until one night he left me bleeding from the throat because he choked me nearly to death and hurt my son.

My minister was a Houston police patrol officer in our area and he took the call. He took me and the children home to stay with him and his wife until we could get a place. He advised me to get a divorce ad he'd seen my husband parked at the house of a woman of ill repute and he said I had a scriptural reason and not let him come back. He knew my situation and that I got in trouble for taking the children to Sunday school as my husband did not want me to go to church. The patrolman was my Baptist minister and they are firmly against divorce but he advised it in my circumstances and said I had scriptural divorce grounds because of where my husband went that night after hurting me.

I had full custody of the children and was staying with my Grandmother who kept them while I worked and I preached on Sunday's where I could. I was in weekend revival out of town and though I had full custody of my children I would allow him to come visit when he wanted to come. My Grandmother never liked me to preach and she let him take them home to Houston that weekend for a week, promising to bring them back.

He never brought them back and when we tried to call the phone had been disconnected and he had moved away, taking my children with him. He left no forwarding address and was then living with a woman that had a very bad reputation of being a woman of ill repute. At that time the law could do nothing since he was the father and could not be charged with kidnapping. I had no money to hire an investigator and no way to find my children.

I was very hurt and heartbroken. I packed my clothes and drove to Dallas to a tent meeting I'd heard advertised. It was the same one where I was healed of the Cancer long before. I went up for prayer for the children and Bro. Allen asked me when my birthday was and I told him. He said I'd have them back on my birthday! Meanwhile, to go out to Miracle Valley Bible School and work in his prayer group that prayed over the requests that came in.

I had a car at that time but no money much except what I had in my billfold. During the offering I put that in the offering as it was not enough for fuel to get very far. Now never do this unless you actually hear the voice of God directing you to as you will end up walking. But I felt so impressed to give my car away to a woman I'd never seen before. I knew if it was not for a miracle I would never see my children again and I wanted to just sell out and serve God. When we do, not necessarily about money but I did not have much of that, but when we dedicate our lives to totally follow God's will and Word we enter a perfect will of God and it's there we see the miracles take place all the time.

The woman I gave my car to had her hands up praying I had no idea what she was praying. But I put my keys in her hand as I knew I could not go to the Valley unless God made the way so no use in keeping the car.

She ran to the front to tell Bro. Allen she was just praying for a car so she could go to church as her children would not take her nor back to the revival but she got a ride that night with some neighbors.

The meeting was over and they were taking down the tent. I was still sitting on the back seat believing God would make a way. A Minister's wife I knew, Sister Skelton, came over where I was sitting to talk with me. I'd slept in her Sunday School room when going to a revival there at their church. They opened it for people to stay that were from out of town and didn't have money for a motel. I don't think churches do that anymore but they used to do it all the time. It wasn't as comfortable as the Hilton but it was a place to sleep.

Traveling ministers did a lot of things back then they would not do today to be a minister. Amy McPherson, that built one of the biggest churches in the world, Angelus Temple in Los

Angeles, slept in chicken coops along the way to preach the gospel when she first started. I'm sorry to say I do not believe there's a minister today that would do that if they had to in order to preach the gospel, or sleep on a Sunday school floor either.

Sister Skelton told me they had a call at the church from someone on the road to the Valley and could not stop at a motel. They wanted to know if there was anyone here that needed a ride there and could help them drive. She asked if I had a way to go and I told her no. She knew I'd given away my car. She said they would be along shortly just wait for them and I had nothing else to do but wait.

I had been in the prayer tent praying over my way to go and that was before I was led to give away my car. I had a vision and it was strange but I told the sister praying with me about it and she said,

"That's how you're going to the Valley."

The vision was very odd, I saw a heavy set black woman holding a baby almost big as she was but he was asleep on her chest and she was holding him like he was a baby. When they arrived it was a white man and a black lady with two children they were taking out to the Christian school at the Valley. I told her about the vision and she said that was she. Her son was asleep and she pulled his head over on her chest and held him like a baby. She was praying at that time they'd find someone to help them drive as back then the motels would not let them stay. So he just kept driving and stopping on the side of the road to rest. She could not drive and could not help him.

I've often wondered if it wasn't a car full of angels because of how it happened. I believe in Angels and I know they are among us.

CHAPTER 10

ANGEL HITCHHIKER

I'm not sure if we picked up the stranger from the road or he was waiting at a truck stop café where we stopped to eat. It could have been pre-planned and it would not surprise me if I had been riding with a group of Angels. I've heard stories told in church by people behind the pulpits that have picked up angels on the road. They got in the back seat and testified about Jesus Christ and when the people looked around, they had disappeared and the car had not stopped. I've heard many of those stories some about John the Revelator that told them who he was.

This stranger changed the atmosphere of the car. It just seemed unworldly like a visitor from another dimension was with us. He sat in the backseat by me and the two teen agers and talked awhile. I was very led by God to tell him he had a call to preach the gospel and he agreed. I asked him if he was then preaching and he said not then. I presumed he was back slid so I asked could I pray for him and he allowed me to do so with a smile.

I was also led to give him my white bible with my name on it in gold. He accepted it, I asked would he preach from it now and he said he would if I would preach with him. So I agreed. The World Wide Web is my mission field as I'm past 83 as I write this book and my car is too old to get around much anymore. It just won't run well. So I stay home and preach on the Internet and I can reach more souls worldwide.

CHAPTER 11

BIRTHDAY MIRACLE

I was going to Bible school and working part time in the office and I was called to the office on my birthday for a phone call. It was my Grandmother and she said she'd tried to call three days and could not get a line though. She wanted to tell me that had the children back so I could come get them.

She told me she had gone to Houston to

try to find them and inquired everywhere she could but found out nothing. She was buying gasoline to go back home and that was in the day when we had full service stations. Someone would come out and service the car and put gas in it, take real money and bring you the change. Quite different than today when we use plastic at the pump and never see an attendant. Those were good days!

She was crying and the man asked her what was wrong? And if you knew Grandmother you know she told him, in detail.

He told her to just pull to the side and wait until he closed up the station and he'd take her to the children. He felt it was the same couple and children that had recently moved in next door. He said this couple abused the children and left them alone while they went out drinking and that the boy had mumps. Grandmother got them and brought them home. And I heard about it on my birthday just like Bro. Allen prayed.

Brother Smith, the office manager was listening and he said to go get them and he'd give me double salary to come back as I was best worker he had and fastest. There was a missionary to Mexico that had left his small trailer there and told them he would not be coming back and to let anyone live in it that needed a place. So I had a home for the children and they had the full church school there for the workers' children. I went back to Texas and took them back to the Valley.

I saw miracles happen at the valley. One was a woman that had meddled in spiritualism and her spirits would talk through her to each other aloud. She had been to every healing campaign there was and had not been delivered. Bro. Allen sent her to the valley for prayer.

This is a rather funny story as all those girls that lived in the dorm wanted to be deliverance ministers. This happened when I was still living in the dorm.

When this woman came they gave her a room in the women's dorm to stay for awhile. She could be heard talking in different voices and these voices would argue with each other. They grouped together to sleep and would not go to the rest room without others going with them. They propped their bureaus up at the door when all were inside as they were scared out of their wits of the devil. It 's funny because they all wanted to be deliverance ministers and were studying to be!

A few of us laughed at them as though you could bar the door to a spirit. Spirits can come through walls as they are not on the physical dimension nor are they physical nor can be. That's what they want, is a body. They want your body!

And if you open the door to the devil by living like he tempts you to live they will come in and you may not get your body back.

The prayer group always met early before breakfast to pray in the chapel and as we were praying that next morning, I felt led to go pray for the poor woman. The others said they would back me up, way way back! But they did go with me. I knocked on her door and the Holy Spirit gave me words to say.

One of the gifts of the Holy Ghost, when we receive the Pentecostal baptism is the gift of knowledge.

That is quite different than the way the psychics work but it is similar. And in that case, when she opened the door, I called her name and not the name she had given there.

The gift of knowledge is to encourage people that God is aware of their problem. I told her I had a message from God for her and the message was that God loved her.

Sometimes love is the besttr healer. She bowed her head and the spirits that had possessed her screamed the most eerie screams I ever heard and left. When she raised her head and hands she was speaking in the true tongue of the Holy Ghost. If you have it you can feel it, there's a witness that it's real.

She went to Sunday School that morning and testified to her healing. The Sunday School teacher said they'd hear of my ministry when I left the Valley but I don't think they ever did it never was that great.

CHAPTER 12

CREATIVE MIRACLES

When Moses performed the miracles before the Pharoah finally released the Israelites, the magicians of Pharoah mocked them and performed the same thing. Then Moses caused lice to form from the dust particles. That is a creative miracle when life is involved, life of any kind. The magicians of Pharoah could not initiate with their magic, life. Only by the creator's power is a creative miracle performed. I know of a few creative miracles I've seen in my own life.

A New Collar Bone

When one of my children was born, he had a broken collar bone. I took him home from the hospital and the very next day some friends of mine from the Four Square Church came by to see me. We put him on the floor and knelt round him. I say that both of the sisters had on pants and wore makeup which, back in those days was a no no highly condemned by the ministers.

We began to pray in our prayer language and touch the baby and you could see the bruise around the break began to lighten. I took him back to the doctor the next day and asked him to x-ray him as he seemed healed. The doctor insisted he could not be but he did x-ray him and called us into his office.

He showed us the two x-rays. One that showed clearly a break in the bone and other showed nothing. He then showed us the picture of another baby whose collar bone was broken and healed and it had a very thin line where the break had been. He explained that was always the case except with my baby he had no thin line, it looked like a totally new bone. He told us he could not explain it but it was true as he held the baby himself at the hospital for the x-ray to be developed or he would believe they had mixed the x-rays.

Flesh Replaced Instantly

Another son had placed his hand on a rusty nail and the doctor had to cut into his hand to cut out the infection and did this a few times until there was a hole the size of a quarter in his hand.

We had just returned from Italy and were visiting my husband's people in Missouri, and were headed for our new assignment in Bossier City, Louisiana. There was a tent meeting going on I heard on the radio I really wanted to attend and it would be on the way down to Louisiana if we took that route. So my husband said he would and he would stay at the motel while I went to the meeting for one night.

My son wanted to go so I took him and my husband had wrapped his hand in bandages before we left and said the wound was getting infected again it seemed and he'd have to have more shots of antibiotic as soon as we reached our destination.

They were baptizing people in a big tub they had under the tent and my son wanted to be baptized. This was one of the very old fashioned meetings that baptized in Jesus Name as the early church did as explained in Acts 2:38 and other scriptures. It has always been the way of those in the East that took students into their spiritual teachings, to baptize them in their name. This meant simply taking the name of the teacher and the teacher taking responsibility to care spiritually for the student. I believe they call them Gurus and Chelas in India.

My son wanted to be baptized and he felt God was leading him to do so. I explained how dangerous it would be as the water was all but black with dirt from the clothing the people wore to be baptized. He was old enough to know what he wanted to do and he insisted God was directing him to be baptized that night.

So I gave in to his wishes and let him go. First I lay hands on him and thanked the Father for his protection over him that he would not be harmed in any way as he desired to serve him. As soon as came out from the baptism I began to take the bandages off his hand as they were darkened with the dirt from the waters. I felt we could go home and cleanse the wound and re-bandage it and trust God as I had already seen so many healings back in my time of ministry on the field and I believed this would be one of them.

When I took the bandage off I looked at his hand and there was no hole there but pinkish shin over where the hole had been like a newborn baby's skin color. It was a creative miracle. I know many will not understand why I allowed this but I had seen so many miracles I would not go against what I did feel the Spirit of God was doing. I do not believe the hand would have healed on it's own but he would have lost it and the doctor in Missouri was quite afraid of that very thing.

A Facial Wound Healed

At the time I had received the Holy Spirit baptism I was working near Houston and living at La Porte, Texas. My neighbor was baby sitting my two young children for me while I worked. On the way I suddenly felt a very strong leading to turn around and go back home as though something was wrong.

I had gone in and sat down on her divan when we heard screams from the back yard. They had bought a swing set for the children and they had begged to use it and so she set it up without putting it in the ground and told them not to swing him. Of course they did and it toppled over. The swing came back and hit my daughter directly in the face.

She ran to the door but something came over me I had not felt before. It was like I was enveloped in a warm, liquid blanket that penetrated through me to the bones. I got up and walked toward the door as though in a trance. I knew what was happening but I was not afraid. I felt such peace as I'd never felt before in my whole life it was like I was under the control of peace, it was the kind of peace

Jesus must have felt when he slept in the boat in the midst of the storm.

Yes, we can sleep in the midst of the storm as Jesus told us,

"My peace I give unto you, not as the world gives unto you"

The peace of God that passes all earthly understanding was upon me and as the woman and her husband who had just come in were screaming at Jesus I walked up, placed my hand on my daughter's head and spoke softly,

"In the name of Jesus Christ!"

And the bleeding stopped instantly. We took her to La Porte clinic and the doctor that put some stitches in her face asked me how we stopped the bleeding. He said if he had been there he could not have done so with his medical skills because of what had been severed. I was very young in the Lord and I did not testify it was God's hand upon her that did it. It was neither me nor the couple but was the hand of Jesus Christ that touched her though me.

That is all Jesus wants, is an instrument to use to perform the miracles he taught us we could do, also, when he said,

"Greater works than these shall you do, because I go to my Father."

Now some teach that the greater works are building of great Cathedrals and monuments but Jesus never built a Cathedral nor a monument. He spent his time healing the sick, casting out the evil thoughts, desires and demon spirits that had inhabited the bodies of others and setting them free. Those are the greater works that he wants us to do in His Name. It is not us nor our power nor our holiness but it is all Him and His power and His holiness that enables us to have the greater works ministry he promised.

New Lung

The accountant at the Valley School was from Bro. Noah's Oak Cliff Assembly of God Church, one of the largest in Dallas, Texas at the time. He showed us a picture of his lungs before and after prayer. He had been given a death sentence by the medical profession as there was nothing they could do for him. He heard of Rev. Allen's tent revival coming to Dallas and he went with little hope but a lot of prayers. Bro. Allen prayed for him and he knew something had happened. He went back to the doctor for another x-ray and he had both x-rays with him he showed to people. The second x-ray showed perfect lungs. That is what we called a creative miracle. Only God can do that.

While at the Valley Bible School, we heard of a measles outbreak in town but few of the children contacted the disease. My daughter began to break out with red spots one morning. I called some of neighbors in, we laid hands on her and prayed, within less than an hour they had disappeared and she had no further problem.

Most of us that went to Miracle Valley were there either seeking a miracle healing or had already had one. It was Bro. Allen that prayed for me when the doctors wanted to do a hysterectomy and introduced me to Pentecost and the ministry of Jesus Christ. Had I not been healed at that tent meeting my last three children would not be here. My appreciation goes to Jesus Christ that paid for the healing on Calvary and Rev. A. A. Allen that had the boldness to do what Jesus told all his disciples to do; go forth and laid hands on the sick in his name and they would recover, and many did.

A criticism of Rev. Allen's ministry is how people that were supposed to be terminal could suddenly get up and run around the tent. In bible days that's exactly how it happened. A man crippled from birth that received his healing got up and ran into the Temple praising God. When there is an instant healing there is no trace of the problem left nor of any of its effects on the body, therefore, the person is perfectly normal and can do anything a normal person can do.

It is no problem for them to get up and run around the tent praising God. It's as though the sickness had never been, their strength is back and they behave like a normal person though some might not think so. But you would run and praise God, too, if you'd been confined to a death bed awhile, too.

In instant healing, no trace of the problem or what it has done to the body is there anymore. That's why some are called creative miracles. There is also the healing that begins with prayer and gradually manifests over time. Those are two different ways of healing. There is a gift of the Holy Spirit called "miracles". This girl is in operation with another gift, called, "gift of healing" when the instant healings occur. However, Rev. Allen did not claim a gift of the Spirit. He simply claimed he believed literally what the Bible said and believed it more than what the devil said. And that is to what he attributed his healings.

As example of this, years later, I was called to go to the hospital and pray for a woman's friend and she did not tell me what was wrong with her. I had no idea she was so near death. She had tubes in her and I could see her bones through the sheet. I laid a little St. John's Gospel on her stomach, placed my hand on it as led by the Holy Spirit to do, and claimed healing in the Name of Jesus.

I then hurriedly left and thought as I walked out of the room, that woman will be dead soon. It was not a mental healing nor a faith healing, it was effected by the healing anointing of the Holy Spirit and my Angels that have been with me in my ministry.

The woman that had called me to go pray for the lady in the hospital was a friend I had met at a revival in Shreveport and I had gone to her home in Mansfield, Louisiana to hold a bible study and prayer meeting. It was about six months after I had gone to pray for the woman in the hospital I kept feeling very pulled towards going to visit the friend in Mansfield though I had not heard from her.

When she opened the door she was very glad to see me, she had lost my phone number and wanted to get in touch with me so she had prayed I would call or come to visit again. That's how the Holy Spirit works.

I thought she wanted me to hold another bible study and prayer meeting for her and told her I'd brought my accordion just in case. She said,

"No, that's not what I wanted. There's a woman wants to meet you. Do you remember that woman I called you to go pray for in the hospital a few months ago? The one dying of stomach cancer? I forgot to tell you they said her stomach was completely eaten up by cancer."

"Yes," I replied, "When did she die?"

"Oh my Lord she didn't die! She came home the next day, and ate fried chicken. She has knocked on every door in Mansfield telling that Jesus Christ is alive today and still in the healing business. She is very much alive and healthy and wants to meet the woman that prayed for her, let's go!"

So we went to see her and she was on the verge of what I would call a bit too pleasingly plumb. She took a hundred dollar bill from a cookie jar and tried to make me take it but I would not. I have never and never will take money for what God does through me.

She told me she owned the building where the black church held services and any time I wanted to come there for revival if they would not let me preach they could stay home until my revival was over. I told her I could not do that to any church but I should have gone back and attended and I'm sure they would have allowed me to hold some meetings.

CHAPTER 13
ON THE SAW DUST TRAIL

Miracle Valley Bible School was not a typical Bible Seminary. We used to call them cemeteries. So many on fire for God went away to the Bible Seminaries and came back backslid, cold or lacking the heartfelt desire to win souls for Christ. I don't know about all Seminaries but some of them were like that.

We learned the dead letter, too, our studies being in the New Testament and the life of Jesus but more than that, we learned to pray, we learned to worship God and about the world of demons. Demons do exist and they can enter in and possess people as they did in Bible days and still do today. There is not much taught about them nor mentioned in the modern churches.

After the Valley experience a sister and I from my hometown went out in the Ministry together. We determined not to tell anyone we were ministers and let God tell them. We never had any trouble in that way as we couldn't hide from them. First church we went to was a little store front church which in that time there were many of them. People rented any type building they could afford, to preach the gospel. The woman minister recognized us as ministers and told us to come up and hold her a weekend revival which we did.

Now I'm not a snake handler but I don't condemn them at least they take all the scriptures literally! But I believe that scripture means a snake can't hurt us if we stay under the umbrella of God in God's perfect will. There are three wills of God mentioned in the scriptures one is the acceptable and that is when you are living on the rim. It's when you are in the perfect will of God you see miracles take place.

We visited another church that was holding service late and were having an old fashioned baptism at midnight in a cow pool out on someone's property. We went and I decided to be re-baptized. I'd had laryngitis and lost my voice and could not preach that night. I was running a fever. My partner said I'd get my death of pneumonia if I went in that cold water.

They were some of the old timey people that baptized according to Acts 2:38 in Jesus Name as Peter did and the minister said I would not as he would pray and the angels would warm the water and he did. It was like going into a Jacuzzi, you could see the steam coming off of the water.

When I came out I was dancing in the spirit, singing in the angel tongue and I fell in the spirit. It was in the spirit thankfully. Not all the dancing you see now is in the Spirit of God. These dance troupes that come in with white robes and some barely dressed are not in the Spirit.

I was looking for some old time gospel singing with the anointing of the Holy Shirit on it and thought surely I'd find some at Lee University, that I believed was sponsored by the Church of God of Cleveland, Tennessee. I remember a great miracle that took place in the Church of God back when I was in the ministry.

One of the dear sisters was pouring hot grease into a glass jar which was not too wise, it broke and splashed all over her arm. In those days we went to the church for prayer or called for prayer before we went to the doctor and many testimonies in the Pentecostal denominations were about healings.

I was called to come pray with them as I went there when I was home and I saw this happen. As we gathered around praying in our prayer language and using the Name of Jesus the blisters began to break and new skin appeared where the burn was. Not completely a healing but it had begun.

When I was dancing after I was baptized, I fell on a bed of cotton mouth water moccasins which are the most deadly snakes there are in Texas. They bite you out of water and there's no hope. I didn't know it as if I had I would not be here, if I'd moved. I felt I way off and I could hear myself singing in tongues. Everyone got deathly quiet suddenly and I wondered if they'd gone off and left me but I just kept singing in tongues. I felt something wet come across my body and move across my throat but I didn't really comprehend it at the time as I was out in the spirit and did not want to come back. I just kept singing in tongues.

In a minute the minister took my hand and pulled me up, everyone started shouting and we went home. No one said anything about it and I didn't think anything about it until we were on our way to Dallas the next day and my partner was driving, thank goodness, as it just dawned on me that was a snake!

CHAPTER 14

GIRL IN THE BLACK SHORTS

When God tells us something he knows what he's telling us. We both prayed and were led to go to Dallas. Before we left, I was praying in my prayer language and I saw a vision. I saw a girl come to a door and she had on what we called back then, pedal pushers, pants that came just over the knees. They were black and she had a cigarette in one hand and a beer can in the other one.

God told me to tell her he loved her. There was so much condemnation preaching in my day and I felt there was not enough understanding of people and their circumstances. You cannot frighten someone into accepting Jesus Christ as Lord. When you tell them of the great love God had for them that Jesus went to Calvary to pay a debt he did not owe for those of us that owed a debt we could not pay, it causes people to want to know about him.

God often gives me that very message to tell people and that's all they need to know about God to make Jesus their Savior and Lord, simply that God loves them. And God loves you that are reading this book, too, regardless where you are or what you are doing, he just wants you to come home.

My partner had a cousin lived in Dallas she said we could go by and stay with them one night but be sure not mention God or that we were out preaching as they'd make us leave. They were God haters and living in the most unholy sins.

We went up to the door and the girl that opened it held a beer can in one hand and cigarette in another and I told her I'd seen her in a vision and God had a word for her. I almost didn't tell her but the spirit was leading me so strongly to do so and I said there was just one thing not right and she wanted to know what it was. I said she didn't have on black shorts as she did at the time but they were pedal pushers down below her knees.

She asked me to touch her leg exactly where they were in the vision and I did. She said wait just a minute. My partner said now I'd done it and we'd be sleeping in the car again tonight! I said I had to do what I had to do. My partner was sure she was going to go get her husband to tell us to go away and not come back. But that was not where she went.

She came back with pants legs in her hand she got out of her trash box. She had cut them off that morning!

She invited us in and as soon as we entered, there was a knock on her side door. It was a little nine year old girl from another apartment there, she asked if we were angels? She told us that she gave her heart to Jesus at a Baptist church but her parents would not let her go back. She had prayed and asked God to send her angels to teach her about him and the Bible and she dreamed about them. One had on a black hat and one a red hat and I had dark brown hair and my sister partner had reddish hair.

We got her down on her knees and got down with her and we looked at each other as we didn't know what to do and we laid hands on her head. She got up raised her hands and started singing in the most beautiful Indian language it sounded like and doing a pretty Indian type dance.

We were praising God and speaking in tongues and there was a knock on the front door. This was another lady from another apartment and she wanted to know if she heard people speaking in tongues there. I thought she was going to complain and I told her yes but we could stop if we were too noisy. She said,

"Oh no, don't stop! You speak the same language my father spoke when he prayed. He was an old time Pentecostal preacher and I promised him on his death bed I'd continue with God but I have not. We found out she and her husband had been a part of the parties there and they changed wives as well as drank and did drugs.

She was crying, the other one was crying and still holding her beer can. We told them we'd find them a church and my partner took the Dallas phone book, went to the church section, closed her eyes, prayed, turned a few pages and put her finger down on a phone number and we called it.

It was a woman minister and she invited us to come preach that night. That's how the spirit used to use people in the ministry now they make schedules through their organizations and they don't think to ask God where to go.

We took them and the way the story goes, the other woman took her husband later and they both accepted Christ as their Savior and finally went out to Mesquite, Texas and started a work. I don't know the name of it I always wanted to go there and see them it could be a big church today I really do not know. The woman's name in the black shorts was Violet. The way her story goes is that her husband would not let her continue in church and brought a man home with him to sleep with her for money. She went in the bathroom and began to pray and she told God he had to help her now. She had not yet received the baptism and she received it with evidence of speaking in tongues.

She went back to the living room speaking in tongues as she could not speak in English. Perhaps it scared them perhaps they understood God and it was a warning but they left and her husband never came back.

She began to take in washing and ironing to make a living for her and her five children and continued in church. A man came and brought his laundry to be done and he had five children and his wife had died. They ended up married and went to Mesquite with the other couple to start a work for God. She was younger than I was and if you happened to be reading this book, Violet, give me a call I'd love to know what happened later to you. I'm back home where I started from.

Chapter 15

MY CROWNING MOMENT

While in Dallas, we attended a healing meeting by one of the ten top Voice Of Healing Ministers of the day, Rev. James Dunn. He had a story of angels. When he was a young boy he fell into a raging river and could not swim. Two Angels rescued him, sat him under a tree and told him they would be back to assist him as he had a healing ministry.

His angels would go to someone in the audience that had the faith for healing and he could see them, and he would call them out and pray for them and usually they were healed.

For protection he would have a group of women standing behind a woman to catch her if she fell in the spirit and some men to catch the men as sometimes people will fake it and sue for damages.

Some have no respect for God. You don't need anyone to catch you if it's the true power of God as the angels make sure you are not hurt. He had my partner and I come up to work with him as catchers and he sent us back to the very back on concrete to show he did not have a battery up his sleeve as some claimed. He also rolled up his sleeves when he ministered.

He pointed his hand at us, spoke in

tongues and we both fell backward. It's like falling into set jello, angels hold you and you do not hurt yourself as you fall backward.

He never let any ministers stay back of him on the platform as he ministered with the angels nor let any stand beside him. The last night of the meeting he had me come up and stand beside him and pray with him for the people. He told me his angels knew my angels and I could stand beside him.

He wanted to take us with him as part of the evangelistic party and flew his wife down from West Virginia to meet us and approve and she did. But the other ministers spoke against it as back then people would have talked about us.

His wife stood up in church and said she knew her husband and that all he did was stay in his motel room and pray or he could not have the ministry he did and she wanted us to go with him to help him but the other ministers convinced him not to do it because of the puritanical attitude of so many. They were afraid it would hurt all our ministries. Today things are very different in the religious world.

CHAPTER 16

LOVE FIELD ORDINATION

We were staying at the Bibleway camp grounds during that revival owned by Rev. Guy Shields. He wanted to take us around to his churches in the organization, introduce us and get us revivals. He had a revival scheduled at a church up north and though he was not well he insisted on going.

I took him to the airport so the car could

stay at the camp grounds. There were several itinerant ministers there that stopped by and spent a few nights on their journey for God. And the staff always fixed something to eat for all. This was not unusual back then as they didn't have big churches supporting them to put them in the Hilton Hotels. They went where the Spirit led them to go and they left healings in their wake. That's back in the time when God was God and Christians were Christians and you can tell the difference.

I drove him to Love Field which was the only field in Dallas at that time and carried his bag in for him. He was about to enter the tarmac and stopped, sat his brief case down and said God told him to ordain me right there now. He was going to ordain us to the ministry when he returned and his Bible College class was graduating. He had a Baptist Seminary at the time in Dallas though they did accept women and ordained women to the ministry. Kathryn Kulhman, the famed healing minister, was a Baptist minister and had a church somewhere up north when she began her ministry. I am not inferring Baptists have all the truth but they do have the born again experience which is vital. It is a work of grace not works and when a devout Baptist received the baptism of the Holy Spirit there's no stopping them as they are not afraid of the devil himself. Most of the modern Charismatic movement have the same basic belief, that we are saved by grace not works.

Right there as people passed us to board the plane he laid his hands on my head and ordained me to the ministry of Jesus Christ. I would never receive another ordination, that was sufficient for me. I will never forget it nor Rev. Shields. He never came back. He died in the pulpit preaching the gospel he loved. He was truly a man of God.

CHAPTER 17

MY ITALIAN MISSIONARY JOURNEY

Back in the early days of my ministry I was praying in my prayer language and the Spirit spoke the word, Italy. I knew one day I'd go to Italy for a missionary work. Later I married an Air Force man and he was assigned to go to Italy.

I didn't know where any churches were and I presumed there was nothing but the regular chapel services. We were at the Base one day and waiting outside the BX, sitting on a bench and a lady came sat by me. We we started conversing and she invited me to the Pentecostal Fellowship. They had no music at the time and I told her I could play if I had the music book. I can read music well and I play church music but I don't play classics anymore as I used to do because of unfortunate circumstances.

So I went and she and I and a black sister from Tyler, Texas got together and moved out to a seashore resort town where we could meet for morning coffee, bible study and prayer. We started a work in our homes each week, and we would direct the service when it was in our home. My husband had some young airmen working under him he would let off to come to my services, they told him they wanted to come to his house as they were better services than they had attended in the States.

Shirley, Inell and I started doing some Missionary work and passing out tracks on the beach to the Italians. We started an Italian work there in my house and first night we have forty Italians counting the children and our interpreter had to work, Shirley's husband was going to interpret for us as he spoke Italian and we did not. Shirley said,

"How are we going to know if they receive the Holy Ghost or if they are just praying in Italian?"

I don't know, I said, I feel we will know the difference though!

After we left Italy, they gave the Italian group a night to meet in the Base Chapel

Rev. Roy Strickland was over the European Pentecostal Servicemen's Fellowship, a great man of God, one of the leaders in the Church of God of Cleveland, Tennessee. He was just an ordinary Christian man with a powerful anointing of the Holy Spirit.

He came occasionally to see about the Fellowship and to preach revivals for us. We stood out in the rain one day passing out invitations to his meeting. I became ill and lost my voice. So I could not talk that night when the service began.

One thing about the old time Church of God if the Spirit of God was not in the service they stopped to find the key as they believe there is a key for every service and it may not be the preacher.

They don't have those kind of services anymore that I know of, they are all planned out before they start. We never had dance troupes back then, if we danced it was in the Holy Ghost. It was powerful and many fell under the power and came up healed of whatever was wrong with them. You don't see that anymore but those days are coming again and a great revival is on the way. The Prophet Joel called it, the Latter Rain.

Bro Strickland didn't seem able to preach through the block so he said someone holds the key to this service and he walked back to me, grabbed me by the throat, rebuked Satan and told him to turn me loose. Satan is the cause of all the sin, sickness, suffering and death on the planet. Adam and Eve were given the dominion and authority of the Father creator and they sold out to Satan, lost the authority and that's why today sin, sickness and death reign in this world.

People often argue over what the original sin was. It does not really matter what that sin was but the real sin was the fact they did not believe God meant what he said. That's a very important to know. Do we really believe God means what he says in the Bible? That is the secret of miracles. To really believe God means what he says and take the scripture into our heart and believe that it is God speaking today and speak it forth on our lips and it will come to pass, in Jesus Name.

He handed me the microphone and said,

"Now preach! You have the key to revival in the Church of God!"

And I did, my voice clear as a bell. There had been a lot of problems as we had every Pentecostal denomination in one group there and it wasn't easy to preach to them as one group would not agree and get mad.

Somehow I did right that night. I just let the Holy Ghost do it and when I did they were hugging each other at the altar and crying and two people we never thought would ever speak to each other were in each other's arms! It was a great revival and I truly enjoyed working with Rev. Roy back then. I believe what I basically said was that God loves us all in spite of our arguing over doctrine and scriptures and if we really have God in our hearts, we will love each other in spite of it, too.

When we took him to the airport to leave he told me,

"Sister Patti, next time I see you, I want you to be a member of the Church of God of Cleveland, Tennessee and I'll help you get an exhorters license and you can preach in any of our churches."

I never did and I regret that very much. He wrote me the nicest letter of recommendation to take to any church where we were stationed. I will always remember the group there and our prayer meetings. We would have prayer requests from different ones that heard about our prayer group.

Our tour there was in early 1970's. We had a nurse friend that came at times and she told us that the Air Force hospital in Germany sent a team of technicians down to see what was wrong with the x-ray machine at the clinic on base as they were sending people up to Germany with tumors and cancer and other things that showed up on the x-rays but they found nothing wrong with them when they got there. They believed the x-ray machine was broken. But it wasn't. They had been through our prayer group either in person or by proxy or request and we had prayed the prayer of faith and God did the rest. Nothing impossible with God.

I'll never forget my friends from the Pentecostal Fellowship at San Vito Air Force Base, San Vito, Italy. The base is now closed but I hope the Italian work is still going on somewhere.

I loved Italy as one of my favorite places to live and I loved the Italian people, and they loved me. They told me they thought I must be Italian and not American as most Americans were not friendly with them and they were a friendly people. I'd go back in a minute if I were young enough to go on another missionary journey.

CHAPTER 18

SHREVEPORT MINISTRY

When we left Italy we were had assignment to Barksdale Air Force Base at Bossier City, over the bridge from Shreveport. My last child was born there and had a broken collar bone. I took him home and the next day two sisters from the Four Square Gospel church that I knew came by to see him. We put him down in the floor, got around him, laid hands on him and began speaking in tongues. We could see the bruises fading away and he didn't cry anymore when I picked him up. I could even pull him up with that arm the doctor said not to touch for awhile until he healed.

So I took him back the next day and asked the doctor to x-ray him again and he didn't want to as he said it would take a few weeks for that bone to heal. But I convinced him to do so and he called us into his office and showed us the x-rays.

He showed us another baby's x-ray that had the same problem and when it was healed it had a thin line where the break had been. On my son's x-ray it showed no thin line and no break at all. That's what you call a creative miracle of God, he had a new collar bone. The doctor said if he had not held him himself to wait for the x-ray to be developed he would not have believed it was the correct x-ray. He could not explain it. I could but I did not because did not think he would believe me. I'd seen those things happen to much back on the saw dust trail of the healing revivals.

Before coming into Bossier City we stopped on the way for an old time tent revival I heard advertised on the radio. My older son had stuck a rusty nail in his hand and the doctor had cut out the infection a few times until there was a hole down into the bone we could see. We kept it wrapped and sterile and he was having penicillin shots.

He wanted to go with me to the meeting and during the meeting they were baptizing people in a big vat and the water was dirty. He had the idea God had led him to be baptized that night and he was determined to do it so I let him. When he came out I took the bandages off and said we will rush home and wash it and you will be alright I know, if God told him to do it I was not going to stop him. I know the voice of God and I felt it was God and God was going to perform a miracle for us and he did.

There was no hole in his hand and only pink skin like on a newborn baby. I was newly created skin that's another creative miracle.

When Moses did his first miracles before Pharaoh the Pharaoh had his magicians duplicate them. But then Moses created lice from the grains of sand and the magicians told Pharaoh,

"That is the finger of God!"

A creative miracle can only be performed in the Name of our God the magicians, the Satanists and the metaphysicians cannot manifest life, they cannot create new life. That is in the hands of our Creator God.

While in Shreveport I met Rev George Dykes and together we started services in his car lot offices and were soon given a building for our group which continue to grow. We called it the "Life Church of North

Shreveport". We had a radio program once a month and held conventions in one of the local hotels. Some came from out of state. We had great services.

My husband received orders for Okinawa, Japan and I had to decide to go with him or stay there in our home we had purchased for less than twenty thousand which was a good price in the mid 70's for real estate. We had a beautiful place.

I received three prophesies in three different churches to remain where I was but I did not listen. I had preached in a small church at Point, Texas and the Pastor told me to come back any time bring my bible and hold services as it was the best service he'd seen and he was Pastor of one the large Assemblies of God in Dallas, Texas until he retired and started the little Assembly of God at Point, Texas. He followed me around playing his guitar and people were praying and out in the Spirit, he just said it was best service he'd been in. He wanted me to stay there and he would help me get places to minister but I decided to go with my husband to Okinawa, Japan. I missed the will of God.

My ministry has never been quite the same since I returned. I did accomplish one thing there I started track ministry with the Bishop of the church of God in Christ and his wife, and the pastor of the church. We went down on Saturdays to BC street which was a very bad place for anyone to go. Our boys had hardly left home and been sent overseas and they went down to BC street and they would be led to get drunk and hooked on drugs and get in trouble with the law. Over there we were under Japanese law.

I attended a baptism of a young boy hardly out of high school that had been given drugs and led to do something bad and he was on his way to a Japanese prison and they told us they were not tall enough for Americans and they could not stand up straight and had to stay at least a year and this boy perhaps a lot longer. He had no one and it broke my heart and that's why I wanted to do the track ministry and save others from the same fate.

At the time, I was going to the white church of God and I'm Caucasian. The licensed Church of God minister that had the track ministry thought was not having any help with it but me, visited us and gave me the tracts he had and anointed me to take over the tract ministry there. I had showed my letter of recommendation from Rev Roy Strickland to the Pastor of the church.

My whole family went and the one with the tract ministry knew my husband and came out to eat with us before he left and give me the ministry while he was gone TDY. He had to go suddenly and he told me to just get up at church and tell them I had taken the tract ministry and wanted some of the young men to go with me to BC Street Saturday as I could not go alone, it was no place for a woman alone.

So the Pastor got up after me and said,

"If anyone feels a call to work for God you can come clean my bathrooms!"

Well, I had said I was called of God to do the tract ministry as a licensed Church of God minister had given me the call. And it was not to clean bathrooms plus he had a wife that should have been doing that. So I asked a black couple that came there where the black church was and they became offended they thought I meant for them to go there and I told them no I was going myself!

So that night I drove down to Naha and it takes a few hours though not that far in miles the roads are narrow there is a lot of traffic and we drove on the wrong side of the street! I got there and the Bishop was sitting in his office with the door open and he called me in asked me what I wanted.

I told him I wanted to get someone to go

with me to BC street to pass out tracts and try to win some of those young boys to Jesus away from that sinful place. He said come on in let me introduce you to the Pastor he just sat here before church started and told me same thing. He felt called to go to BC street and rescue some of the innocent boys that are being lured into giving all their money to the prostitutes and getting into trouble.

So he stopped the service and took me into the Church of God In Christ which I am still a member of, they anointed me as Missionary of the church. So that Saturday, Bishop and his wife, the pastor and I went to BC street. We started going to other churches and talking to them about going with us and when I left Okinawa we had three church bus loads of Christians going to pass out tracts and witness to our young servicemen.

When we got back Stateside our home that my husband decided to sell against my judgment and warning, that we made a few thousand on selling it for twenty five thousand dollars was on the market for one hundred and ten thousand dollars. I never had another home. But I'll have a brand new home one day when I get to go live next door to Jesus. I'm looking forward to that day.

CHAPTER 19

MINERAL POINT MIRACLE

When my husband retired from the military we moved back to his home in Missouri where he was from. I felt led to drive out Cadet and Mineral Point, where he was raised, looking for a little country church to work in. I spoke to two elderly black ladies sitting on their porch and stopped to talk and asked them about a church in the area.

They said the county had given their people a church but they had no one to preach in it and asked if I was a minister and I told them yes I was and looking for a little church. So I opened the church so they would have a place to come worship God.

Tornadoes were bad in the area and one night had a severe storm and was under tornado watch. I had them get up and begin to worship God for protection, I don't teach anyone to pray like some used to pray. God has already done all he's going to do it's up to us to appropriate what God has already done through Jesus Christ at Calvary. So I teach people to just thank God for what the Word says is already a finished work at Calvary.

I gave a prophesy at the time through the Spirit that no tornado would come passed the city limits of Mineral Point. My husband was in attendance and heard it. A few years later he was visiting with hi mother in Springtown and he watched a tornado coming down the highway and turn at the Mineral Point road. Usually a tornado will not change its course unless it runs into a river or another road that crosses its path. There was no road or river between there and Mineral Point so it was evident that tornado was going right through the main street and take that little church down.

I was visiting some of my children in Texas at the time and he called to tell me about it. He was never much of a believer in my ministry nor my prophesies so he said he got in the car and followed it to see all the destruction in Mineral Point.

He got to the city limits sign which was still standing and right in front of it was a deep ditch that tornado had dug as though it hit a solid wall it could not go through. It veered off into the woods without hurting anyone. I don't know if there has been one since but that one could not pass the city limits and he remembered my saying that no tornado would get past the city limits of Mineral Point.

I'm past my eighty third birthday now and the only mission field I have is the world wide web. You can find me on Face book with my scripture teachings and the websites that will be advertised there. I've seen God do great things in my life time and like my great great grandfather who baptized over 3000, 2000 of his converts he didn't think were ready, said on his deathbed he'd missed his calling, he should have evangelized instead of being a circuit Pastor and founding churches. He founded over a dozen churches now taken over by the Southern Baptist Convention and there are two books with chapters on Rev. Asa K. Routh in their main library.

CHAPTER 20
THE RAINBOW BRIDGE

I was sitting in my recliner one night as I was healing and it was hard to get around to do things for myself, and I talked to Jesus, I said if I am not going to be able to get do for myself and to get out anymore and do for the Lord then I'm ready to come home. I asked that I not be left here when I can no longer care for myself.

Instantly I was out unconscious, not asleep and I was standing at one end of a beautiful rainbow bridge. You can consider this a vision or an actual what is called "astral" projection of our Spirit... we are not our body, we are Spirit, made in the image an d likeness of God as God is not a physical man but Spirit as Jesus told us. Otherwise he could not live in our hearts. A physical being could not come into our body and dwell with us as Jesus said,

"The Father within, he does the works." And,

"Of my own self I can do nothing, the Father within does the works"

And he told us the Father would be in us, and that's what it's all about. The Spirit of the Father within us. In the beginning, Adam and Eve had the Presence of the Father with them and in them. We are both In Christ and Christ is in us. This is a great mystery hid from generations now revealed unto us that believe in Jesus Christ. "Christ in you, the hope of glory." (Colossians 1:26-27)

Mankind lost the Presence of the Father because of sin and through Jesus Christ we are restored into that Presence… "We have been delivered (through Christ) from the power of darkness and translated (back) into the Kingdom of the Son of God…" (Colossians 1:13)

We used to sing a song in our church in Shreveport in the mid 70's I co-pastored with Rev George Dykes that went something like this:

"Restoration started at Pentecost restoring to man what Adam lost."

Does your church not teach that through Jesus Christ we are restored back to the dominion and authority that Adam and Eve were given in the garden before they sinned? Then find you one that does because you are not receiving the spiritual food for your soul to grow in Christ.

As I looked to the other side of the bridge it was such beautiful scenery as I've never seen and we've traveled in three continents in my lifetime and seen some pretty country. It was a woods area as I've always told God I don't want to live in a city I want to live in the country where the deer and birds, squirrels and other animals can be safe and come eat out of my hand. I love animals and I love the country and the woods. And this was exquisite woods. It looked as though it was kept by a gardener. It had exotic green foliage and blooming flowers all through the trees.

I started to step up on the bridge and suddenly Jesus appeared and held his hand out for me to stop. He said,

"You will come to me, but not now. Go back, there is a work for you to do."

I believe that my work today is on the world wide web where I have a ministry site and post teachings on my Face Book page.

There are no churches today like we used to have and no Holy Ghost services where we saw the signs and wonders of the ministry of Jesus Christ. There are psychology lectures and self help teachings from the pulpit and I don't like to sound like what we used to call "a clothes horse preacher". But there are women ministers today that wear what some would feel indecent wearing in their bedrooms.

When tight pants give the appearance of being the flesh whether it is material or not, to wear behind God's Holy Desk I do not believe proper. I know I won't be appreciated by some for saying this and some will call me an old foggy but I was one of the most modern ministers of my time. I wore pants on the street which was then a no-no but I would not think to wear them behind the pulpit today. The difference in mens' trousers is they are not tight fitting nor show their nakedness which the tight fitting pants of women do.

I truly hear a lot of noise but I do not feel the old time power that performed the miracles I've seen in my life. But I believe I will see it again as it's coming. There is coming the greatest revival this world has ever seen. Joel's army is preparing to rise with the signs following their ministry they had in the days of the Christ. The Bible prophesies it and almost all the prophesies have been fulfilled but the great wave of the Latter Rain outpouring of the Holy Spirit is yet to come but it's on the horizon.

And the great revival will not come through the ministers and pastors of the great churches of the country but from this revival will be a revival of the Saints, those that love God and are sincere with God will be filled with the supernatural power and miracles, signs and wonders will again fill the earth once more before the time of the end.

When I was in Italy I had a vision one night. I was kneeling by my kitchen chair praying and the Angel that has been with me all my life picked me up and took me into the spirit realm and I could see through my kitchen wall the Adriatic sea. We lived in a seaside resort town but I had no window facing the sea and only a wall but I could see through the wall and I saw Jesus walking on the water. His hand was outstretched, the hand of mercy but it was slowly closing into a fist of judgment. As Prophetess Ellen White once said, he is fixing to get up take off his prayer robe and put on his war clothes and when he does we better be ready.

I won't close this book without offering my readers a chance to accept Jesus Christ as Lord and Savior. The word used for salvation in the New Testament is "sozo" which means far more than salvation of the soul. It means healing for the body. The Finished Work of Jesus Christ was as much for healing of the physical body as for cleansing of the soul and bringing one back into fellowship with your creator.

It was not our creator that wanted Jesus to suffer. It was our Creator that took a human body and went to the cross with your sins, your karmic debts and mine in our name. He did not have to die he was Immortal but he died in our name so we might live unto God.

According to Romans 10:9-10 if you believe in your heart that God raised Jesus from the dead and confess him with your mouth as your Lord you will be saved. Remember saved is more than your soul, it's your physical body from sickness, disease and yes death itself. Paul saw a group that would overcome the last enemy he called, death, in the last days. We are in those days and the Spirit is looking for that group that will believe the literal word of God and not try to spiritualize it or make a metaphysical statement out of it but believe God meant what he said.

They fight over what the sin of Adam and Eve was in the the theological circles but who cares what it was. It was not what they did but the fact they did NOT believe God meant what he said.

Do you believe God meant what he said?

Think about it. Your future depends on the answer.

Amen

ABOUT THE AUTHOR

The author was born in Sulphur Springs, Texas where she graduated from High School in the National Honor Society and attended Texas State Teachers College. She Dedicated her life to full time Christian ministry at First Christian Church summer camp. Ordained by the late Rev Guy Shields founder of Bible Way Fellowship and Bible Seminary in Dallas, Texas.

While on tour with her Air Force husband, was active in missionary work in Italy, establishing an Italian mission in her home that was later incorporated into the Chapel. While on Okinawa, Japan she began a tract ministry with two others that grew to three church bus loads of Christians participating. While on Okinawa, the Bishop of the Church of God in Christ ordained her as Missionary Evangelist.

She co-pastored the Life Church of North Market Street, Shreveport, Louisiana, with Rev George Dykes in mid 70's; Pastored a full gospel mission at Mineral Point, Missouri in early 1980's. She studied for the ministry at the Miracle Valley, Arizona Bible Academy in early 1960's and traveled the saw dust trail during the healing wave of the late 50's and 60's, preaching and praying for the sick wherever she found an open pulpit,

Missionary Evangelist Spencer is great-great grand daughter of one of the early Pioneer Baptist Ministers,

Rev Asa K. Routh, that converted over 5000 in the horse and buggy days as a circuit Pastor and established over a dozen churches that are now a part of the Southern Baptist Convention. Now retired and living in her home town, at age 83 her mission is now the world via Internet where she posts her ministry teachings on her websites and her scripture messages are found on Facebook.